Looking
Forward *to*
Sunset

KIRK *and* JODI BACON

WESTBOW
PRESS®
A DIVISION OF THOMAS NELSON
& ZONDERVAN

WestBow Press books may be ordered through booksellers or by contacting:

WestBow Press
A Division of Thomas Nelson & Zondervan
1663 Liberty Drive
Bloomington, IN 47403
www.westbowpress.com
844-714-3454

ISBN: 978-1-6642-6393-2 (sc)
ISBN: 978-1-6642-6395-6 (hc)
ISBN: 978-1-6642-6394-9 (e)

Library of Congress Control Number: 2022906986

Print information available on the last page.

WestBow Press rev. date: 04/25/2022

Now unto Him who is able to do exceedingly,
abundantly above all that we ask or
think, according to the power that worketh in us.

—EPHESIANS 3:20 (KJV)

In 2017, I started having health issues. I was experiencing shortness of breath, dizziness, and fatigue, and I almost blacked out a few times. Tests were conducted. I received a diagnosis, and then I lost my job of over twenty years. All of a sudden, I had no way of continuing any treatments or follow up appointments. When the problems persisted, finding another job just was not going to happen. We decided that a change in lifestyle was necessary.

We moved to Belize and bought a café.

One Year Later

July 23, 2019. I remember bits and pieces of walking from one pillar to the next and leaning against each one. Blurred people walked by. I was very tired. My feet felt like they were made of concrete. I could not catch my breath. I remember seeing passport machines, then walking up to airport security. Next, I was being guided through a scanner and I could not lift my arms. Then I was led to a chair and a conversation took place, but I do not remember what was said. Then paramedics were saying I could go on to Oklahoma or go to the hospital. Next, I was on a gurney being wheeled through the airport. Paramedics surrounded me and I was put into an ambulance. I remember someone saying that I would get a headache and then a warm sensation started from my feet and moved up my body. Suddenly, it was like a light switch flipped and everything was just gone.

The next thing I remember was hearing my name. I was on a second story deck looking out at the water, leaning against a white railing. It was a beautiful view and I was thinking, *Wow, we made it!* Then I heard my name again, asking me to do something. I woke up wondering how much time had gone by. I was angry that I was no longer looking at the water, and wondered what happened to the house with the balcony. I felt like a failure here, but not there. I did not understand why I was back. Nothing made sense.

I heard two voices. One was my wife Jodi and the other was a woman I did not recognize. There was excitement in their voices.

Chapter

I t's difficult to know how to begin to explain this journey we have been on. We were finally living life and living our dreams after raising our five kids. It was just the two of us again. We were living in paradise and had a small business that was ours and very special to us.

Kirk and I witnessed some of the most beautiful sunrises and sunsets. Many mornings, when we rode our bikes to work, we watched the sun come up over the ocean. We would often just stop and look. We took pictures, but none of them could ever capture the real beauty before us. Many evenings we looked toward the west side of the island as the sun was setting. The colors in the sky were always breathtaking; no two nights were ever the same.

Then God abruptly put a halt to all of our plans and said, "Do something different." I felt him speaking to my spirit, saying, "What you have done for the past year was important and has a purpose, but there is something more important that you need to do instead. Do not worry. There is a reason for all that I am allowing you to go through, just trust me. I am going to teach you and use you both in ways that you never dreamed were possible."

To share our testimony, I must start when everything changed.

In March of 2018, my husband Kirk lost his job of over twenty years. He had been having health issues and was referred to a cardiologist. The doctor ran numerous tests and finally came back with a diagnosis. We would later learn that this diagnosis was only a tiny issue and not the full extent of what was going on.

When Kirk lost his job, which by itself was devastating enough, he immediately lost his health insurance. He was still in need of procedures but could no longer get them.

His job was the primary source of income in our home. I worked part-time in retail.

We were given instructions on what to do at home to help him feel better. He needed to start using his CPAP for his sleep apnea, and he needed to continue to take blood thinners. He had been diagnosed with polycythemia vera. We later learned that it was the secondary form of polycythemia, which was the noncancerous version. It basically caused his blood to be thicker than normal, which made his heart work harder.

Let me just say that, at the moment of his diagnosis, he was extremely tired and under heavy stress at work. He worked between forty-eight and sixty or more hours per week and did so with swollen legs and feet, shortness of breath, and chest pains. We thought there was more to it, but we listened to the doctors.

Kirk followed most of what his doctor had told him to do. He took daily blood thinners and always used his CPAP; he chose not to have phlebotomy treatments due to his extreme anxiety over needles. He was told they would help him feel better quicker, but it was his choice.

We were at a crossroads. What now? We had visited Belize several times over the previous two years and had fallen in love with the island of Ambergris Caye. We had already booked another trip there for June. Since it would probably be the last time we could visit for a while, we continued with our plans to go. Our oldest daughter, Emily, her husband, Brent, and our granddaughter Piper, who was two at the time, would be joining us along with our youngest son, Garret, and his wife. Our youngest daughter, Sarah, decided to surprise us and tag along too. Kirk and I have five kids, three girls and two boys. All of our girls are married and have given us seven grandbabies so far.

We cashed out Kirk's retirement with plans to use it until he found a new job and then reinvest the rest into something new. That something new ended up being a small café and bike rental shop in San Pedro, Belize. We had always dreamed of moving there when we retired and felt like it was the right decision for us.

The entire process was effortless. Things fell into place so easily. We were beyond excited. Three weeks after we returned home from our family vacation, we were packed and ready to move. We were moving somewhere beautiful, and we could live a much less stressful way of life. Things were very laid back in Belize, very relaxing. We decided we could be more physically active and spend our free time riding our bikes on the beach. In fact, they quickly became our main transportation everywhere. We could also eat healthy foods. We ate lots of fresh fruits and veggies, chicken, and seafood. Food in Belize is mostly locally grown. We both noticed improvements in how we felt. All the sunshine and fresh air was an added bonus.

It was also the first time since before the kids that it was just the two of us. Our youngest son stayed in our house in Oklahoma, and we made the move with just ten bags. Most of the contents were supplies for the café and Kirk's tools. We learned that we needed very little to be happy. Our happiness came from being together. We also enjoyed phone calls with our family, cooking for people, and visiting friends and people who rented our bikes. We met people from all over the world in our little café.

Our first year in San Pedro flew by. We made some wonderful new friends and shared some unique experiences with them, like the golf cart Christmas parade. Everyone decorated their golf carts with Christmas lights and tinsel, then joined in the local parade and gave away tons of candy to the kids. We ate Thanksgiving dinner with our close friends at a restaurant owned by friends from North Carolina. We constantly made plans to improve and expand our business, and we learned so much along the way.

As much as we treasured our time in Belize, we also looked forward to our first visit back home to Oklahoma. The trip was planned for July. Our youngest daughter would be visiting too and bringing our new grandson August, or Gus. Kirk's brother, Frank, and his family would also make their annual visit. We would have all our kids together and get to see extended family.

We had missed a lot, being in Belize that year. A month after we moved, my mom and dad celebrated their fiftieth anniversary. I hated not being there, but I still helped with some of the planning. At the same time, our daughter Kimberly was due to deliver our fourth granddaughter. The day of my parents' anniversary, I FaceTimed our son Garret at the party so I could see family and friends. This happened to be the day that I found out my dad was having heart issues. He was going in for a procedure the following week. That planned procedure rapidly turned into a quadruple bypass. I desperately wanted to be there for my mom, but with a new business, it was just not possible. I messaged and called a lot, and our oldest daughter, Emily, was there for my mom when I couldn't be. On February 10, our youngest son, Garret, turned twenty, and August, our first grandson, was born in Alaska. But traveling that far was impossible for us.

Excited was not a strong enough word to describe how I was feeling about going home. We had two grandbabies to meet and parents to hug, with extra hugs for my dad. Knowing that I could have lost him made me want to hold him just a bit longer than the rest. I was literally counting down the minutes.

We decided to close the café for ten days. It was a slow season in San Pedro, so it was the perfect time. Our daughter Kim and her husband, Joshua, had given us one-way tickets home. We would wait until we were home to purchase the return tickets in case we needed to delay a day or two. The plan was to return on August 2, the day before my birthday.

About a week before our trip home, Kirk and I went for a ride on our bikes up the beach. We were going to spend some time outside visiting with our friends Rob and Krista, who own a bar and grill on the beach. On Friday evenings, they had trivia. Kirk and I played many times, and we were terrible at it. We started going and listening to the game, trying to answer a question or two on our own. We also enjoyed the fresh air and moonlight over the water. We stayed for a couple of hours and visited with Rob after the game. We rode our bikes back down the beach to return home. It was about a mile each way.

The ride was usually an easy one. That evening, however, Kirk had a lot of difficulty. We had to stop a couple of times to rest. When we finally got home and inside, he was having a hard time catching his breath. I looked at him, and he was drenched in sweat and pale. He said his chest hurt too. It eased his pain to hold up his left arm, but he was so tired that he could not hold it there for long. I held it up for him, and after a few minutes, he seemed to be okay. He was just very tired. I spent the evening on WebMD and Kirk came in to try to rest. It was a very long night. He had chest pains throughout the night, but they finally let up around 3:00 a.m. He was exhausted for the next few days.

Two days after this happened, some friends came in for breakfast. I was telling them what had happened to Kirk, and our friend Kimpi, who had just had a cardiac procedure, said that those were classic symptoms of a heart attack. Down deep, I knew that she was right. She offered to give us a ride to the local doctor in town who she knew; after some debate, Kirk finally agreed, even though said he was fine.

Doctor Rodriguez, a very nice older female doctor, did an examination. She also did an EKG. Everything, including the EKG, came back totally normal. She wanted to do blood work as well, but it wouldn't be back until after our trip and it was expensive. All of the medical care in Belize was out of pocket for us. She suggested that it was probably just really bad acid reflux, which can mimic a heart attack sometimes. We knew that was not the case. Kirk had dealt with acid reflux for years. Since she saw no red flags, we felt some peace about making the trip home. We decided to go to the VA (Veterans Administration) while we were in Oklahoma and get him checked out again just to be on the safe side. Kirk is a retired Marine, but we had never needed to use the VA for medical care until this point.

We left Belize the morning of July 23. We had a three-hour layover in Houston and were scheduled to arrive in Tulsa around eleven that evening. It was a beautiful, sunny day. Our dear friend Bob drove us, in his golf cart, to catch the water taxi to Belize City. Once there, we took a cab to the airport and ate lunch. We both were looking forward to seeing everyone and had been talking about the items that we needed to make sure we picked up while in Oklahoma to bring back to Belize with us.

Chapter

The first flight lasted two and a half hours. While in the air, we both rested and played games on our phones. Kirk had been looking forward to getting a burger in the Houston airport, so that was our plan during our layover. We had one piece of checked luggage, Kirk had his backpack, and I had a carry-on bag. With bags in hand, we exited the plane. We followed the crowds leading us to the passport scanning stations.

It was at this point that I noticed Kirk was having difficulty. He walked from pillar to pillar in line, leaning against each one. He said he felt tired and out of breath. We slowly made our way through. The next stop was to pick up our checked luggage. We needed to take it to the domestic baggage area. Kirk was getting really tired, so he sat down on a bench, and I waited for the luggage in the international baggage claim area. Once I had the bag and wheeled it to where he was sitting, I asked if he was ready to go. He reluctantly agreed. At this point, I was starting to worry. He didn't usually have this kind of trouble just walking through the airport. It only took a couple of minutes to get to airport security. However, before we got in line, he needed to sit again. We had plenty of time. There was no need to rush.

I said, "Do you think you can just get through this line? Because then we can go get some food and rest a while before the next plane."

He agreed and we stood. We walked to the station where they scan your ticket and passport, and he said, "I don't think I can go any farther."

We had only walked about twenty steps. The lady who scanned our information asked if something was wrong. I told her he was having trouble breathing. She asked us to wait a minute. She went somewhere, then rushed back and walked us past all of the people in line straight up to the scanning station where we had to put our belongings on the conveyer belt. Kirk started complaining of chest pain again. He was sweating profusely too. He went into the scanner and could not hold his arms up when asked to. Someone got him a chair, and I followed him through the scanner as quickly as I could and gathered our belongings.

A man came rushing up behind us. He told us that he was a paramedic from Belize City and had been on the airplane with us. He happened to be walking behind us and noticed that Kirk was having trouble and wanted to help. He asked an airport employee for aspirin and for the location of the defibrillator in case it was needed. He assessed Kirk and stayed with us until the emergency responders arrived at the airport. Once they arrived, they moved Kirk and me over to a bench farther away from the security area so we were out of the way and there was more space to better take care of him.

Several EKGs were performed on Kirk. They all came back normal; however, his pulse was racing. He was also very pale and continued to struggle to catch his breath; the chest pains continued.

The paramedic who performed the EKGs told us that it was up to us if we wanted to go to the hospital or not. After a few minutes, Kirk was beginning to feel better, just like he had a few days before. Kirk looked at me and told me that it was my decision to go home or to a hospital.

At that moment, the chief of the paramedic crew looked at me and said, "Ma'am, I have been doing this for over twenty years. You need to get him checked out."

That was exactly what I needed. Someone needed to say yes, it is serious enough to go to the ER (emergency room). We agreed to go; Kirk was strapped to the stretcher and taken outside of Houston Hobby Airport, where there were two ambulances parked. For some reason, that same chief stopped one set of paramedics from taking us and had another set take us instead. He instructed the second team not to go to the usual hospital, but to Memorial Hermann Southeast. I had explained to him in the airport that we were uninsured, with the exception of Kirk's VA plan. He assured me that where he was sending us to would take excellent care of Kirk, no matter what the circumstance. I now believe that God was directing this man to take us to the exact place that Kirk needed to go. God had a plan in the works.

Off we went. The paramedic gave Kirk nitroglycerin after telling him to let it melt under his tongue. Kirk asked if it would make him go fast. Oh how I needed to laugh right then. We arrived at the ER, and he was immediately taken to have another EKG. It was about 10:30. I asked to borrow a phone, because our phones would not work in the United States. A nurse offered me hers. I called my mother from a phone number that she would not recognize. I asked her to please call Garret and tell him not to go to the airport to pick us up. I went on to explain that Kirk had been taken to the hospital with what they thought might have been a mild heart attack, but we were still unsure. I told her that we would most likely be kept overnight and be on a plane sometime the next day. She agreed, and we hung up. Two things I knew for sure at that moment: my mom would call Garret and, more importantly, she and my dad would pray. My dad is a pastor and they had been serving God longer than I have been alive. We trust and know in situations like these to turn it over to God.

By this time, Kirk and I were both hungry and tired. Nothing moves quickly in the ER. We waited several hours for the hospital to confirm it was a heart attack. The troponin levels in his blood rose with each test. This, we were told, is how they confirmed a heart attack. We waited even longer for the hospital to approve his admittance. Finally, I was able to use the hospital WiFi and my cell phone through Facebook messenger to give my family updates.

The plan was for him to have a heart catheterization procedure sometime the next day, or rather that day, since it was after midnight. Kirk's nurse brought us sandwiches once we settled into a room and we tried to get some rest. When I woke up, I spoke with my brother Eric, who happened to be traveling and was in Houston. He came by and spent a few hours with us. We had not seen any of our family in a year, so his presence was a great comfort. Shortly after he left, they came to get Kirk for the procedure. I was shown to a large waiting area. The technician told me the procedure should take about an hour and a half to two hours.

I messaged the kids and let them know what was happening. I asked Garret to go to my in-law's house and explain to them what was going on. With family visiting, they could all be informed at one time and there would hopefully be no confusion. After that, everyone just waited for the updates. I was anxious and called one of our daughters to fill the time. Finally, after two and a half hours, someone came out to talk to me. They said that everything was finished and that someone would come get me within the next few minutes.

I would be taken to Kirk and they would explain what all they saw and did.

Another hour passed before a nurse took me to Kirk. I was shown to a computer screen where I viewed the blocked widowmaker artery on the left side of Kirk's heart. It had been 99 percent blocked and was now flowing normally thanks to two stents. Kirk was awake and alert and listening to one of the nurses tell him a story about something. At the same moment, the doctor was explaining to me that Kirk would be taking an anti platelet medication as well as various other new medications. He made sure that I understood that he had to take the Plavix twice daily and only one aspirin or the aspirin would work against the Plavix. He also told me that if he quit taking it for any reason for at least the first year, or started skipping doses, that it could literally kill him. After watching Kirk first in Belize, and then in the airport, I knew that nothing was more important than keeping him healthy.

Kirk was upgraded to an ICU (intensive care unit) room. Once he was settled, we called the kids. He would be monitored for the next twenty-four hours and, if all went well, he would be released the next day. Our sons Jake and Garret decided to drive from Oklahoma to see us; they were worried. We tried to talk them out of it since we would be seeing them in a day or two. They insisted, and headed our way that evening. Kirk and I spent the rest of the day just relaxing and watching television. We went to bed early, knowing our sons would be arriving very early the next morning.

3

Chapter

We woke up around four o'clock the next morning. It was now July 25. We cleaned up a bit, but did not have much with us since our clothes had gone on to Oklahoma. Luckily, our son-in-law, Brent, was able to retrieve our luggage from the Tulsa airport and deliver it to my parents' house. The kids were bringing us a change of clothes. At about 4:30 a.m., our sons arrived. We were so happy to see them. We hugged and talked and hugged them some more.

We went to the waiting area and got some coffee, and brought Kirk a cup too. We were all in the room visiting. I was talking to Garret. Jake and his dad were having their own conversation.

All of a sudden, Jake shouted, "Dad," and shouted a second time louder, "Dad!" Then he ran into the hallway and yelled for help. I turned to see that Kirk's coffee had spilled into his lap. His eyes had rolled back and his chest was jerking up and down a bit but there was no breath. Jake quickly came back followed by a team of nurses. Then they did something that shocked us all: they called a Code Blue. I never expected to hear those words in person, and I certainly didn't think it would happen to my husband.

We watched for five long minutes while they worked to bring him back to us. He was rushed back to the heart catheter lab, where they discovered that one of the stents was blocked. I now understood what the doctor meant when he said that, without the medication, he could die. They discovered that Kirk was part of a very small percentage of people who are Plavix-resistant. His medication was changed to Brilinta. So far, there has been no history of anyone being resistant to it.

We went back to his ICU room. We were relieved but also very shaken up. After this scare, our second oldest, Kimberly, her husband, and their three daughters, decided to also head to Houston. At this point our family started to see that this was much more serious than we first thought. Kirk's brother Frank and his family also headed our way. They all arrived in Houston the evening of the twenty-fifth, but went directly to their hotels to rest; all of them planned to see us the next morning. Garret had to work the next day, so he headed back to Oklahoma, while Jake remained with us.

Late that evening, Kirk and I had our first moments alone. There was no family, doctors, or nurses—just us. We only had this privacy because he needed to use the bathroom and I stayed to help him. I was so grateful, because I needed his comfort and to fall apart for a minute or two. Sometimes you just need your spouse to hold you while you cry. I had no idea that this moment would be the last time he would hold me in his arms for a while. With tears in my eyes, I told him how much it scared me. He looked at me and said, "Don't worry, stop crying. I'm not going anywhere." He had tears in his eyes as he spoke those words to me. I knew it had an effect on him as well. My husband is not one to show his emotions easily.

The rest of that day passed quickly and soon we were ready to sleep. The nurses brought in a Bi-Pap machine for Kirk to use since his CPAP went to Oklahoma without us. Earlier that day, Jake was playing some Third Day songs in the room, and they were still playing in my head that evening while I drifted off to sleep.

Around 1:15 in the morning, I woke up to use the restroom. On the way back to my chair, I heard a noise coming from Kirk's direction. I walked over to him and put my hand on his chest, and he opened his eyes. I asked him if he was okay, and he said yes. I asked if he was sure and he said, "Yes, I'm fine." I sat back down in my chair and as soon as I reclined in it, I heard the noise again. I shot up, knowing something was not right. My instincts were correct. He was coding again!

I ran for help, and then watched as the hospital staff descended on the room. This time, twice as many came. Once again those words Code Blue were spoken. It was 1:20 a.m. I was terrified and alone at the hospital. Jake had left for a while and nobody else had come yet. I cried and tried to pray while watching teams of nurses take care of him and try to bring him back to me. Two large male nurses took turns doing chest compressions. I later learned that they rotated twenty-seven times. They checked his pulse and there was none, so they shocked him. With no pulse found, the compressions continued. I was taken outside of his room and given a chair. I could still see and hear everything because the wall was glass and the door remained open. The hospital chaplain came and stood with me.

Suddenly it hit me—they were preparing me to watch him die! I called several of my kids and only one of them answered. It was our youngest daughter, Sarah, who was staying with my parents. While I was talking to her, they checked his pulse a second time and there was still none, so they shocked him again. I remember telling Sarah that I didn't think her dad was going to make it. At some point Tami, my sister-in-law, called too and I told her what was happening. They were at a nearby hotel, so they quickly headed our way. Jake came back during all of this and we just held on to each other for dear life. Finally, after twenty-five minutes, with one final shock, they got a faint pulse. He was back. He was awake and fighting them a bit, so they sedated him. I felt numb. This was like having a nightmare that I could not wake up from.

After this traumatic event, a team of doctors came in to talk to me. They had no answers as to why this had happened again. They had just taken him back to see if there had been another blockage, but there was none. The plan was to keep him sedated and monitor him closely. After the discussion with the doctors, Kirk's brother Frank and his family arrived at the hospital. Kirk was unable to communicate with anyone. We took a trip down to the café and got coffee. It had been about two years since we had seen each other, but we could only manage small talk. Tami, my sister-in-law, is a nurse. She was able to explain some of the things going on in the room with the monitors and some of the things the nurses said to each other that were foreign to me. We all watched as Kirk continued to twitch and shake, and the nurses and doctors worked tirelessly to try to stabilize him. There was nothing to do but watch, cry, and wonder what was going to happen next.

After their visit, at 9:02 a.m., Kirk coded for a third time. Once again, I watched it all, and so did Jake. It was terrible! This time, Kirk bit almost through his lip and tongue. The room filled with staff again, and Jake and I held each other with tears in our eyes. It was such an incredibly painful thing to witness, and it just kept happening. This was my husband, the love of my life for thirty-three years. Jake and I stood in almost total silence while the nurses put a breathing tube down his throat. They shocked him three more times, over a sixteen-minute period, before they once again brought him back. It was overwhelming. Why was this happening?

After that third code, they really struggled to keep Kirk stable. A doctor told us that the hospital had no way of helping him any further. He went on to explain that Kirk's body was in, what he described as, an electrical storm. Kirk needed to be transferred, as soon as possible, to the medical center in downtown Houston, where they were better equipped to handle complex patients like my husband.

There were problems though. Because we were uninsured, there had to be special approval to transfer Kirk, and a doctor at the medical center had to agree to take on his case. He also had to be approved for life flight, because he would not survive the ambulance ride. Finally, there needed a to be a bed in their cardiac ICU unit and at that moment, one was not available. Kirk had died three times in less than twenty-four hours. He needed to be there yesterday. I called my mom and asked her to pass on the news asking everyone to be praying. She shared with our family and put us on our church prayer chain.

Our daughter Kimberly showed up around this time and ran to her daddy. He was heavily sedated, but she held on to him, cried, and told him how much she loved him. Next she came over to me and I wrapped my arms around her. We both were crying, but I was grateful. I needed one of my girls with me. We are all very close. She and Joshua brought to me a little bit of joy in the midst of the sorrow—actually three little bits of joy in the form of three granddaughters. God gave me a way to rejoice when my heart was breaking. I was able to meet our newest granddaughter Noelle, and love on her and her big sisters, Faith and Sarah Grace. God was there and brought me what I needed when my world was crumbling.

God answered our prayers very quickly. Within two hours, everything was approved and arranged. We were told that we would have to take a taxi to the other hospital once the life flight crew arrived. Jake and I went to catch a cab, and Kimberly and her family went to have nap time before meeting us at the other hospital later. Before leaving, a nurse took off Kirk's wedding band because his hands were swelling. Jake brought it to me. I happened to have my grandmother's silver chain on and I quickly hung his wedding band on that chain around my neck. It would remain there until it could go back on Kirk's hand.

We arrived at Memorial Hermann Medical Center and were instructed to go to the cardiac wing, then up to the fifth floor where the cardiac ICU unit was located. At this point, the rest of our kids were on their way to us and would arrive later that day. Once we were on the fifth floor, we asked about Kirk but there was no information. Frank and his family were there with us. Kimberly and her crew arrived shortly thereafter, and Garret had returned. After a couple of hours, we were all getting anxious. Jake went to see if he could find out anything about how his dad was doing. He was brought back to the waiting area, and we were told that someone would be out to talk to us soon.

Chapter 4

Another hour or so went by. Finally, a nurse took me, alone, back to see Kirk. I met the doctor who was in charge of his care. When Kirk had first arrived, they immediately took him to surgery to install the Impella pump. It is a system used to pump your heart for you. It entered his body through a main artery in his right inner thigh area. The surgery was successful, but once I was in the room, the attending doctor was having a very serious discussion with the team of doctors and nurses surrounding Kirk.

He finished his talk and then turned to me and introduced himself. Doctor Johnson explained the procedure to me. He explained that although they were hopeful that the Impella would help to stabilize Kirk, it had just not happened. They were still doing everything in their power to help him, but so far nothing was working. He then explained that they had one last option—he referred to it as a "last ditch effort." The plan, if I agreed to it, was to add the ECMO (extracorporeal membrane oxygenation) device. It would be placed like the Impella, but on the left side; it would pull the blood from his heart and oxygenate it, and then pump it to the vital organs. They were hopeful that these two devices would work together to stabilize him. Kirk was also in complete renal failure. He was placed on a CRRT, or slow continuous dialysis machine, as well.

The doctor asked me if I had family with me and I said yes. He then looked directly at me and said, "You realize how serious this situation is, right?"

"Yes," I answered.

He went to explain that the procedure was very high risk and that Kirk could very easily die. Then, he asked me if I had any questions for him.

I asked, "Is it possible that Kirk will not come off of these machines, even if you are successful?"

Once again, he looked directly at me and answered with honesty and compassion. "Yes, it's likely he won't."

Knowing there were no other options, I signed the paperwork for them to move forward with the plan, and then went back out to the waiting area to let the family know what was happening. We sat mostly in silence. While I was in that room with Kirk, I couldn't even touch him. I wanted to so badly. I just wanted to let him know I was there and that I loved him. I felt like I was being torn apart.

About an hour later, the rest of our family—Emily, Brent, Piper, and Sarah—arrived. Finally, all of our kids were with us in one place. Sarah's husband Jayden would be joining us the following day. He was on deployment in Korea, but was already on an emergency flight headed our way. The only one not present was our grandson Gus, who had stayed in Oklahoma with his other grandparents.

Each reunion was bittersweet. I was so grateful to see and hug each of them, but on the other side of that joy was just pain. It had been a year since we had seen each other. It should have been an exciting reunion, not one filled with tears. However, through it all, there was peace. That kind of peace only happens by knowing God. It made absolutely no sense, but peace filled the waiting room. The Bible says that He is our very present help in time of need. That is the truth and I felt it in every moment.

Another hour or more passed, and finally a doctor came out to where I was talking with Emily and Sarah. He let us know that the ECMO was successfully placed, and that he was now semi stable. He also told us that Kirk had coded a fourth time while in surgery. We were elated that he had made it through and was still with us. I asked if we could see him and was told that he was still in recovery, but that someone would come get us once he was in his room. Finally after more waiting, a nurse came out to get me. I asked if Emily and Sarah could see their dad before they left. She hesitated, but I let her know that it had been a year since they had seen him. All of the other kids had seen him, and they needed to see him alive before leaving for their hotels for the night, just in case they didn't get another chance. She agreed, and Frank, Kirk's brother, asked to join us as well. The nurse let us know that he was still extremely critical, and that we had to stay quiet and not touch him just yet. They were having such a hard time stabilizing him and didn't want to do anything to stimulate him in any way.

We followed the nurse through secure doors and down a long curved hallway lined with rooms with glass walls on both sides. His was the last room on the left, room number 516. We entered a scene that none of us was really prepared for. His bed lay perpendicular to the couch that would soon become my bed. His head was towards the glass wall. To his left side, starting at his head was the ventilator, breathing for him. Farther down by his left arm were three or four IV trees holding what had to be at least twenty different bags of various medications. At the foot of the bed was a hypothermic machine. They had placed him in a hypothermic state to slow his body down so it could have time to heal. To the left of it was the ECMO machine. It had an oxygen tank strapped to the side of it and there were two tubes as big around as my index finger going from the machine and were literally sewn to his inner thigh and into his body. Next to the ECMO on the right was the Impella pump. The tubes from it were not quite as large and running up his left leg, but also sewn in place. Both legs had circulation boots that would inflate and deflate regularly. On his right side at about shoulder height was the dialysis machine, and there were about twelve gallon-sized bags of dialysis fluid hanging from it. The dialysis connected to Kirk through an arterial line in his neck. The left side of his neck had another catheter called a swan. His mouth had a breathing tube of course, and because of his mouth being open, you could see how severely swollen his tongue was from the bite. His lip was also swollen and blue. His arms both had IVs and had blisters.

A nurse was moving quickly around him. She was working quietly, trying to get everything in order. Her name was Sonny. She introduced herself to us, and I let her know I would be staying in the room with him once the family left for the night. She allowed us all to spend only five or ten minutes. There was a heaviness present in that moment. Both of the girls just looked at their daddy in stunned silence. Frank looked at his brother and shook his head, later telling me that he was the older brother and it should be him going through this, not Kirk. Kirk is the youngest of five. His brother Frank is the second oldest. There are ten years between the two of them, so I understood where he was coming from.

We exited the room. Back in the waiting area, we said our goodbyes for the night. I let everyone know that I would inform them of any changes through the night. I prayed that there would be no need to. Once they were gone, I headed back to the room. My bag was there, along with a second bag of things the girls brought me.

A nurse brought me some sheets, a pillow, and two blankets. The room was so cold. Up until three days ago, I had been living on a tropical island. I was no longer used to the cold. We rarely used our air conditioning there, so I was freezing. There weren't enough blankets in the world to warm me that night. But there was peace in that room, even with the chaos of the machines. I felt that peace to the depths of my soul, but I was at a total loss for words. I tried to think of what to pray, but was at a complete loss. As I sat on the bed, I was reminded of a song from earlier, "When the Rain Comes," but it felt too sad to sing. I just got quiet for a few minutes and the Holy Spirit began to minister to my brokenness. My thoughts somehow came back to Kirk's wedding ring that was hanging from my grandmother's necklace around my neck.

My Grandma Murphy had a hysterectomy when my mother was a little girl. The hospital sent her home, but she did not stop bleeding. She was taken back to the hospital but was growing very weak from the amount of blood lost. A man there donated his blood to try to help save her life. Even with that, she grew weaker still. She was becoming so weak and unresponsive that a nun came in, prayed for her, and read some scriptures from the Bible about the blood of Jesus. My grandmother, unable to speak, remembers in her spirit, crying out to God to heal her by His blood. A priest came in and gave her last rites because they did not expect her to live through the night. Sometime during the night, my grandmother woke up in her dark hospital and witnessed the brightest light in the corner of her room. She said she felt love and healing. She knew God had heard her prayer and that she would live. She did live, for many more years. She lived long enough to tell my mother the story, and for my mother to tell me as well. It is a testimony that has been passed down in my family, and was just what I needed for such a time as this. Something that God had done over sixty years ago, before I existed, had a direct effect on this exact moment for me. Even though my grandmother is now in heaven, she left behind such a treasure. What God does in our lives are things we should all treasure.

In that moment, I remembered a Third Day song. I knew that the Holy Spirit was directing me to what I needed. I began to pray these words over Kirk, with my right hand tightly clutching both Kirk's wedding band and my grandma's silver necklace.

> Show me Your glory.
> Send in Your presence,

I wanna see Your face in this God
Show me Your glory.

I lay down on my side facing Kirk. I fell into a peaceful sleep with the sounds coming from five different machines that were keeping him alive.

5

Chapter

When I woke up early the morning of the twenty-seventh, I met our day nurse Maurine. She was awesome. She was about my age and was from Canada. She had been working there for four or five years. I asked her how many people in Kirk's condition did she see live through it. I had told her what the doctor had said the night before. She told me that in her time there, she had only seen two people who were on both ECMO and Impella leave the hospital alive. She also told me that the unit we were in was the unit that people from all around came to when there was no hope. Kirk was in the ward for patients with no hope and these machines were a last ditch effort to save him. I didn't see much hope at that moment. Somehow, I still boldly told her that he was going to walk out of there. She smiled and nodded. I don't know if I even believed my words right then.

I sat back down on my bed after folding up the blankets neatly. I opened my phone to lose myself on Facebook for a few minutes, needing to escape my thoughts. I saw that I had a message from an old friend. She and I had not spoken in years. I opened it and read her words.

> Thinking and praying for ya'll this AM. God led me to this passage and I know you are passing through a valley, but your strength is in your anointing and He will deliver you and Kirk stronger and more blessed than ever before. Love you sister and we will continue to stand with you in belief.

I opened up the picture that she had attached to it. It was of her open Bible. Around these verses, she used her phone to draw a green heart so that I would know what she had read.

> Blessed are those whose strength is in You
> Whose hearts are set on a pilgrimage;

As they pass through the valley of Baka

They make it a place of springs;

The Autumn rains also cover it with pools.

They go from strength to strength,

Till each person appears before God in Zion

Hear my prayer, Lord God Almighty

Listen to me, God of Jacob.

Look on our shield, O God

Look with favor on your anointed one

Better is one day in Your courts

Than thousands elsewhere. (Psalms 84:5–10a CSV)

These words spoke directly to my heart and they arrived just when I needed to hear them. I read them over and over, allowing the words sink in to my spirit. I wanted to call her right then, but instead I messaged her back with my thanks. I also included that I believed that we would have an awesome testimony when it was over—and I believed that we could. But the reality of the situation was literally lying on the bed in front of me. I remembered the nurse's words, and began to doubt. This is where they send people when there is no hope. I knew that I did have one thing to hope in. My hope was that God would answer my prayers and the prayers of the army of people who were praying with me.

I got up and went out of the room to get some coffee and a bite to eat for breakfast. Nobody was at the hospital yet except for Jake, who was asleep on a couch in the waiting area. The family would be arriving soon. I took the elevator from the fifth floor down to the second where a small café called Reds was located. I also remembered it was our granddaughter, Sarah Grace's, third birthday. I walked down to the gift shop, picked out a gift, and then got my coffee and a muffin.

As I approached the elevators to go back up to Kirk, I overheard two women behind me talking. One said, "Oh it's judgment day!"

I turned before the elevator and looked at the two of them thinking I couldn't handle hearing about judgment right now. I said, "I don't think I wanna get on the elevator with you two."

One replied "Oh, it's not your judgement day, but it's a day of reckoning." I just silently got on the elevator, anxious to hurry back to Kirk.

The other woman stood next to me and she quietly asked, "You got someone here?"

"My husband" I replied.

"He gonna be all right?"

"He's died four times, but God brought him back every time."

She said, "That's what God does!"

"I know," I quietly answered, with tears welling in my eyes. Right as I was about to step out onto the fifth floor, she touched my arm and I turned to her.

She looked directly at me, pointed her finger, and boldly stated, "You watch! You watch what God does!"

Up until that point, her words had been soft and kind. The words spoken had authority and absolute surety. I literally felt the words as she spoke them. I had goose bumps on my arms and felt an excitement enter my being. From that point, my heart totally believed God would heal Kirk. My head took a little longer to catch up.

As I approached the waiting area, I saw that a few of our family members had arrived. Jake was awake and they were all talking. I told them what had just happened in the elevator. My son-in-law, Brent, stood up and hugged me. He saw that I was visibly shaking. A few minutes later, the girls arrived and shortly after them, Frank and his crew, followed by Kimberly and her family. With each group that came in, I repeated my elevator story. Some believed and were excited with me; others were probably doubtful. That was okay; I just knew that I needed to share it with them. God would show them what he was up to in His own way.

We all sat together in the waiting area. I decided I needed to have a talk with them. First, I let them know that we were going to begin rotating spending time with Kirk. I wanted everyone to have time with him, but only two were allowed in the room at a time. I explained that everyone would get a turn, and that nobody could go in a second time until all of the others had their turn first. I just wanted everyone to spend time with him and for nobody to feel left out.

For some reason, I also decided that it was important to talk about how we would handle things should Kirk not come off the machines. I truly believed that God would heal Kirk. I also knew that ultimate healing would mean death. We went over how we would approach that if the time would come. Everyone agreed and respected my wishes. When that conversation was completed, I asked Emily if she wanted to see her daddy first since both she and Sarah had only had five or so minutes with him.

We made the journey back to the room and spent a few minutes with Kirk. She was able to hold her daddy's hand and talk to him this time. It was daytime and the window was open, so it didn't seem as sad in the room. We talked a little to Maurine while she looked after his needs. After our visit, I asked Sarah if she would like to go next.

Sarah entered the room. Much like my visit with Emily a few minutes before, Sarah quietly held her daddy's hand. She had also brought a small red and black plaid blanket that belonged to our grandson. She wanted to leave something of his with her daddy just in case Kirk never got to meet Gus. We talked a bit more with Maurine and, after a few minutes, I asked Sarah if she was ready to go. Right as we were about to leave, I turned to Kirk and said, "Okay sexy (my nickname for him for the past thirty plus years), we are going to go, but I will be back soon."

At that moment, Kirk suddenly opened his eyes. It startled me. It was so unexpected that I just said, "Kirk?" His eyes looked straight at me. I said, "Do you know who I am?" He shook his head yes. I instantly had tears in my eyes, and so did Sarah. I looked at our nurse Maurine and said, "He's awake."

She came to his bedside, grabbed his right hand, and said, "Mr. Bacon, can you squeeze my hand?" Kirk squeezed her hand. She repeated the same with the other hand. Then she asked him to move his feet and he was able to move both feet. His blood pressure jumped up after that and she had to sedate him a bit to keep him stable. What had happened was everything to Sarah and me. He had been dead for close to an hour all together, and when that happens, often you lose many things, like the ability to communicate. Kirk followed commands and recognized me. He was still in there and I was overjoyed.

Sarah and I practically jogged down the hallway to the waiting room to tell the family what had happened. Frank and Tami were the next ones to go see him, and he responded to them as well. What a joyous day, and what an amazing miracle that God had just done for our family. We all got to "watch what God did!"

Do you think that maybe God had a plan, that maybe he had organized it all for such a time as this? I believed that with every fiber in my being. The rest of the day, we had an overwhelming sense of God's presence. We all took more than one turn with him and I spent time in between celebrating Sarah Grace's birthday with her, her sisters, and Piper. Having our four granddaughters with me that day was just the icing on the cake.

That evening, once everyone had gone back to their hotel rooms, I just sat in our room in awe of all that God had done in just one day. The kids had blessed me with a new comfy outfit, and had taken me to have a shower at one of their hotels. I was relaxed and at peace and wondering how I needed to share such a miraculous day with all of our friends and family. I decided that I would sleep and then update everyone in the morning.

6

Chapter

The following morning, I walked down to get breakfast. I was pondering how I wanted to word my update to everyone. There was so much to tell that I didn't know how to condense it down for a Facebook post. I sat down at a table. The area was pretty deserted. It was a Sunday morning, so I knew that whatever I posted, most people probably wouldn't see until after church. As I sat there thinking, I suddenly realized that it would be easier to just go live and tell them what happened. So that's what I did. I wanted people to hear from my mouth about my elevator experience and then about Kirk waking up, not hear it secondhand. I wanted them to hear me when I expressed that God had done a miracle, and that I was in awe of Him and so grateful for the power of prayer.

There have been over 900 views and many shares of that video. I did not share it for our benefit at all. I shared it for the glory of God. I wanted people to hear part of our testimony and see what God does. Some of the facts are a bit jumbled together. Anyone who has been through life-altering events will understand that it is hard to keep some facts in order in your mind. In this book, they are in the correct order. I made sure to review all of my journal entries, text messages, and the hospital records themselves. Someone made a comment about Kirk dying seven times and those words stuck in my mind. I just repeated them at the time. Later, I just couldn't remember that many codes and decided to look into it. I went through hospital records, and reviewed the CPR reports. I witnessed three, and Kirk did code a fourth time while in surgery having ECMO installed. Although in the video, I state that Kirk died seven times, that was incorrect. He only died four times. You might wonder why I am concerned about the number. I want to be the most transparent that I can possibly be. I want our testimony to be accurate and only filled with the facts in the best way that I can present them. I believe that it is a miracle for someone to come back to life even one time. For Kirk to have coded four times, and come back all four times, is still an overwhelmingly amazing miracle. Stories told should be truthful. God is a God of truth, and I would be doing Him a disservice by not correcting my own words.

After I had completed the video update, I decided to go back to the room and watch our Oklahoma church's service. They live stream every Sunday, and I just needed to feel that connection to home. I especially looked forward to hearing my daddy's voice. He has been preaching in our church for over twenty-five years. Whenever God is at work, we should prepare for attacks of the enemy. I was operating on autopilot most of that time in the hospital. When I sat down to watch that Sunday morning, there was an attack.

I sat down to watch the sermon, and I heard the words, "I don't know why you are watching that; it's a bunch of lies anyway." I was so desperate for connection to home, and I was angry that anything would attempt to disrupt that time. However, in the midst of the false words, I heard some dear friends tell my dad from the sound booth that I was watching. I then heard my dad say, "Hi Jodi," and then our daughter's best friend yelled, "We love you." It was exactly what I needed in that moment, and God knew it. I messaged my mom about what was happening and asked her to pray. She and I prayed and peace filled the room again. It is important to understand that we have the authority to pray against those attacks. God will hear our prayers and answer.

Over the next few days, the doctors came in and evaluated Kirk, and each day adjusted the ECMO so that he was slowly being weaned from it. They watched closely to see if he would remain stable. After just four days, the plan was to remove ECMO. The kids had all missed work, and had been valiantly dealing with little ones in hotel rooms and hospital waiting areas. They were completely drained. I told them that it was okay to head home. We all knew Kirk would live and that what was next would be a long process. The morning of the July 30, everyone said their goodbyes and headed back to Oklahoma.

Once they were gone, I was completely alone. That afternoon, I went up to the surgical floor waiting area while Kirk was having the ECMO removed. Once there, I sat alone for a few minutes. I was going back and forth from looking at my phone to staring out the window in tears. There was a woman, about my mother's age, sitting near me and she introduced herself. Her name was Paula. Her husband had been having heart issues for years. They had been there numerous times, and he had undergone many procedures. That day was somewhat of a routine for her. I noticed that like me, she had her husband's ring on a chain around her neck. Hers was gold. Mine is silver. She was a wealth of information—the perfect person to talk with. We talked until her husband was out of surgery. She told me that if I needed anything, they were just down the hall from us. I was welcome to come and find her anytime. She also told me that she never went to the hospital without her Chardonnay, and that she would gladly give me a glass if I needed it. I was good without it, but it did make me smile.

Once again, God met my need, before I could even ask for it. He continually orchestrated each day and the people who were around me. Kirk came through the surgery with no complications. It had gone so well that they planned to remove the Impella pump the following day. That surgery went perfectly as well. Paula kept in touch with me throughout those few days. She was a great support to me and gave great hugs.

August is the eighth month. The number eight represents new beginnings. Kirk's heart was beating on its own that first day in August and I was grateful. Any time they wanted to take another machine away, it was okay with me. The ventilator was supposed to be the next to go, but Kirk had developed a septic infection and had pneumonia as well. The evening of August 1 was difficult. We had a new night nurse and it did not go well. Up until this night, Kirk had nothing but the best care from a rotating team of various nurses. This was not the first time we had somebody new come in. That was a constant. This was the first night that his care was lacking.

She was young and very thorough. She technically did a good job, I suppose. The problem was her lack of compassion or understanding for the situation. It was the night that Kirk was scheduled to be bathed. She stripped him of his hospital gown and placed a small towel over his private areas. She then left the room for a few minutes. She did all of this with the curtains wide open and my husband was on full display from the hallway, like in a picture window. She had left the sliding door open about halfway and the lights were all on.

When she came back into the room, I was so angry that I had tears in my eyes. I calmly asked her, "If this was your family member, would you leave them so exposed?"

She flippantly said, "Oh, does that bother you, sorry." She then shut the curtain. I told her that if he had been awake, he would have been furious. I do understand that it is a hospital, and they see bodies in various states all of the time. This was the first time someone had been so neglectful of Kirk, the person she was supposed to be caring for. She didn't speak for a while.

That changed around one o'clock in the morning. She and another male nurse were having a full conversation about the past weekend and their upcoming plans for over an hour. The problem was that the conversation was taking place about two feet from where I was attempting to sleep, and they still had the lights on. They also spoke with normal voices, not even attempting to be quiet.

The next morning, our nurse Desi arrived. She took one look at me and knew something was wrong. I told her about the previous night and she jumped into action. She understood what was needed and talked to the charge nurse. I was reassured that Kirk would not have that nurse again. I was so relieved.

It was August 2, the day before my forty-eighth birthday. I cried a lot after the kids left. Between them going home and the careless nurse, I was a mess. What was the reason for my tears? I had tried my hardest to hold it all together while everyone was there, and now I could finally just fall apart. God saw my needs every day, and before I could even pray and ask for help, He sent something to show me how He was always there, that I was never alone, and that He loved me.

On a wall in the room, various nurses and nurse assistants would fill out the dry erase chart every day with their names and contact info in case they were needed. This particular day I was still feeling down. Part of it was the lack of sleep. I looked up and the nurse assistant for the day was Jesus. Literally, that was the name on the board. I knew he was a young, Hispanic man and not actually Jesus, but it sure made me smile.

I really wanted Kirk to come off the ventilator for my birthday, but after the respiratory doctor came in, he confirmed that it would be a few more days. The nurses had gotten together and bought me a birthday card, and a bunch of them and a few doctors signed it. They also brought me a small crystal guardian angel that I hung in the window by my bed. This wasn't the only angel that day. Jesus was no longer the nurse assistant; I now had Angel. I jokingly told her that Jesus had left me an angel in his place. In reality, I knew that all of these small things all were a part of God's way to show me that He was still there.

I had been craving pepperoni pizza, so I went down to the cafeteria to buy myself a birthday dinner. There was just one big piece of pizza left and it happened to be pepperoni. I also got myself a piece of carrot cake and then went back to the room to enjoy my birthday meal with Kirk. He was getting his dinner through the tube in his nose. I was so grateful though, because it could have been a very different birthday. God had let me keep the gift that mattered most to me on this earth: my husband.

That night's grand finale was in the form of our night nurse. We had never had her before either, but Desi had introduced her, and said, "You will love her!" Her name was Chi Chi, and Desi was right: I did love her. She was from Nigeria and was a strong Christian. We spoke a bit throughout the early evening, and I told her all that had brought us to where we were. At one point, she stopped me mid-sentence and said, "As Christians, we pray and ask God to do something and when we don't see Him answer right away we take it back." Then she looked at me and added, "Quit taking it back, God already has the victory!" God had sent her alright, and I really needed to hear those words.

She spent the night singing songs over Kirk while we both slept. I drifted off to sleep with her beautiful Nigerian accent singing "How Great is Our God." What a blessing.

Chapter

God was showing me in numerous ways that He was going to heal Kirk, and that we would have a testimony. He had shown me over and over that He was there for me. He took care of both of our needs throughout all of the days we were in Texas. Each time He showed me He was there, I was encouraged, and then I would look at Kirk, with my very human eyes, lying in that bed, and I would take some of it back. God was trying to teach me to walk by faith and not by sight, and I was finally starting to let that truth sink in. These lessons can be painfully slow at times.

What I should have done was pray, give it to God, and then praise Him for what He was going to do next. Was I ready? Ready or not, God was going to keep moving and something big was going to happen. I needed my praise to be louder than the words of doubt. I have learned throughout my life that when I am down, or broken, or at a loss for words, good praise and worship music will rally my spirit and keep my focus on God. The words to so many songs ministered to me while we were there. For two or three days, I would place my hands on Kirk's chest and sing/pray the words, "Take this heart and breathe it back to life." Words from "The Hurt and the Healer" by MercyMe were the perfect prayer some days. Other days it was "Whole Heart" or "Another in the Fire" by United. Music has always been an important part of my life, and when I needed it most, these songs that God inspired didn't fail me.

On August 6, they allowed Kirk to be removed from sedation and the ventilator finally was removed. He was finally awake, was able to speak immediately, and was very, very thirsty. From this point forward, there were daily improvements. I finally felt like he was really with me again. We could finally talk, and he had tons of questions. This is when I realized he had no idea of what had happened, no memory of even leaving Belize. He didn't remember the heart attack or the airport or any of the craziness that I had been traumatized with. He was in absolute shock when I told him that he had died four times and come back. He said that his last memory was being in the café and then he just woke up in the hospital. Later small bits of memories came back. I would also soon learn that he experienced things that I was totally unaware of.

Many of the things I told him when he first woke up had to be repeated. Some things I told him over and over for several days. Some things I still have to remind him of. He was trying to sort through a lot of thoughts and feelings. Trying to think clearly when you are in pain is difficult. He was still on pain medications for the large hematoma that the removal of the Impella had caused. He also was still coughing up a lot of bloody mucus left behind from the pneumonia and the breathing tube. He was also treated for pancreatitis. His discomfort was constant. It was a true blessing when our daughter Sarah and her husband Jaedyn brought our grandson August to finally meet us before they had to fly home to Alaska. We spent two days with little Auggie. What a lift to Kirk's spirits he was. Watching the two of them smile at each other with their matching dimples was pure joy to both Sarah and me.

Kirk had also started physical and occupational therapy. This was very difficult for him. He suffered from severe vertigo-like dizziness when he tried to sit up. It made him physically sick; also his blood pressure jumped up and his heart raced. It was so hard to watch my strong husband be in such a feeble place. I knew how overwhelmed he was, and that this was not okay with him. Slowly, over several days, he was able to sit up, for longer and longer periods of time. They had him stand twice, but it completely exhausted him. It's amazing how quickly your muscles waste away when you are on life support.

He was still on the dialysis machine. The renal doctor informed us that his kidneys were just not coming back. It looked like dialysis would be a permanent fixture in our lives. I hated it for Kirk, but it was worth it if it meant that he would stick around. The medical center decided it was time to send Kirk back to the first hospital where he had been. It made no sense to us and I was frustrated. Kirk was not fazed at all. He simply said, "Whatever. It isn't a big deal." My husband had changed in ways that I did not understand fully yet. So I calmed down and started to pack up all of my things.

Two things of great significance happened on August 15 before we were transferred back to Memorial Hermann Southeast. First, the renal doctor came by to see us and told us that we needed to insist on having the perma-cath installed when we arrived at the other hospital. Kirk was having major problems with the arterial lines in his neck and a perma-cath would be a much better solution for the dialysis until they could get approval for a port.

The second thing that happened was the meeting with a very specific doctor. The first doctor I met with when Kirk was life flighted to the medical center was also the last doctor that we saw. We didn't see him even once in between. It's kind of strange how that worked out. He entered the room with his team and my heart pounded with panic. All of those emotions from that first evening he spoke to me came flooding back. He was the one who told me that it was very likely that Kirk would not come off of all of the machines, and that I needed to have my family hurry and get here. He was the final doctor we saw at the medical center before leaving. We had come full circle.

He entered the room and said, "Hi Mr. Bacon. I know you don't remember me, but I'm Doctor Johnson." He shook Kirk's hand, and I looked at him and said, "I do."

He nodded and said, "Yes, this was a much better outcome than we were expecting that night. I'm glad it didn't end the way I thought it would." He spoke for a bit more and then left the room. I explained to Kirk who he was and the role that he had played in this crazy roller coaster we were on.

About an hour later, Kirk was transported by ambulance back to Memorial Hermann Southeast. I had no idea how much I had missed being outdoors until we exited the hospital to get into that ambulance. It was about a thirty minute drive, and I sat in the front with the driver. Once we arrived, we were taken up to the new room. Suddenly, the thought hit me: this is where I had watched Kirk die, more than once. Once more my heart pounded. Right down the hall from us were some of the very people who helped bring him back to me. I was shaking. Why had God brought us back to this hospital? At this point, I knew that there was a plan and purpose for all of it. I just wondered what it was.

The next morning, the various teams of doctors began making their rounds and we were asked the same questions over and over. Our main thought was that we needed the kidney team to come in so that we could tell them what we had been instructed regarding needing the perma-cath. When the new renal doctor arrived, he asked us some questions; one was if Kirk was making any urine. He was, but it was a very small amount. He also looked to see when he had last had dialysis, and it had been the day before. He decided, since Kirk was making some, that we would give his body a break and see what happens. (Watch what God does.)

I had asked our prayer army on Facebook to focus their prayers on his kidneys a few days prior. Over the next five days, every single day, Kirk's urine output doubled and the toxin levels in his blood dropped by a full point. Every day, the kidney doctor came in with a huge smile on his face and gave us the update. On day five, he finally said that Kirk's kidneys were fully functional and the blood work was all at a normal level. We already knew that God could do miracles, so we were not surprised that He had shown us another one. Our nurse told us that day that he had never in all of his days as a nurse, seen a person's kidneys recover as quickly as Kirk's had.

Kirk had also continued with therapy during those five days, but made very little progress. The doctors were talking about a discharge soon and I was wondering how that was going to happen with him still not walking. His muscles were so weak. The plan was set in motion for him to be discharged on August 19. We were very excited about finally going home to Oklahoma. I had no idea how we were going to work out all of the details.

We were told that Kirk would have to enter an in-house therapy clinic in Texas for three weeks before going to Oklahoma. I would not be permitted to stay there with Kirk and had nowhere in Houston to go. Kirk flat out told them that they were not going to separate us. The next hurdles were that he would be required to wear a life vest and would have to pick up all of his prescriptions from the hospital pharmacy before they would agree to a discharge. I tried to go to sleep that night, not knowing how we were going to come up with a thousand dollars overnight. I pulled up Facebook, and saw that there was a fundraiser site through them. It just kept showing up on my page. I decided that maybe this was God's way of providing, although I am sure that Facebook would not see it that way. I said a prayer and set it up. Then I went to sleep, or I tried to anyway.

Nights were difficult after the transfer. First, Kirk had decided that he could get out of bed on his own to use the restroom and ended up sliding to the floor and having to call a crew to get him back in bed. That was eye opening for him. That was when he realized, and so did I, how very long of a road we still had to travel. He would cry at night. It was not like him to cry, not ever. In the over thirty years that we had been together, I had only seen him cry three times. This was a different type of crying than I had seen before. He would hear certain songs and just sob. When I tried to comfort him, he would stop. He never explained why, and I decided not to ask. I thought it was probably about the condition his body was in and the long list of new limitations.

The day before we were scheduled to leave, someone came to fit Kirk with his life vest. It is a portable EKG and defibrillator. Since we were uninsured, we had to pay a five hundred dollar deposit. I looked at the Facebook fundraiser and saw that in twelve hours, it had raised nearly two thousand dollars for us. I had set the goal for five thousand, after figuring our immediate expenses and the bills that were still due and would continue in Belize. By the end of that fundraiser, the goal was reached.

I told Kirk about it and were both blown away. There was an overwhelming feeling of love and support from so many family and friends, and even from total strangers. I called and paid the life vest deposit. After that I went to pick up the nearly five hundred dollars' worth of prescriptions for Kirk. We had money left to cover our very basic expenses and the bills for our café for the following three months. What a tremendous relief, as well as an answer to my prayers.

Chapter 8

All that we had gone through came rushing back to me. Like the EMT from Belize who had just happened to be with us at the airport, and how our entire family happened to be visiting Oklahoma at the same time. I thought of my brother and how he just happened to be in Houston that first full day in the hospital, how I just happened to grab my grandmother's necklace and put it on, even though I was wearing sweats and a t-shirt. I thought of the way God had sent two ladies to that elevator to give me a message directly from Him, and giving a friend words of wisdom to share with me the same day. I continued to see how His hands moved through Chi Chi, the nurse who told me to stop taking it back, and the other nurses who rallied around me on my birthday. I remembered how the name Jesus was on the board and then it changed to Angel. I thought of the amazing care that Kirk had received throughout everything, and the fact that we were in one of the top hospitals in the nation for ECMO. I was amazed at how it felt like we had been there forever, but we only spent twenty-seven days total between the two hospitals. To top it off Kirk, had woken up that first time on the twenty-seventh. God had choreographed a beautiful testimony for Kirk and me and we would not soon forget a second of it. We "watched what God did" and we were, and are, in awe of Him.

On August 19, 2019, Kirk and I left Houston, Texas with our son Garret. Kirk was able to take a step from the wheelchair and into the car, but the effort wore him out. I was nervous. He hadn't been able to sit up longer than about three hours prior to leaving. Now he would have to sit for eight or nine hours. The difference was that he wasn't sitting in the hospital; we were going home, and Kirk was determined to get there. We did make one stop in Dallas on the way. Kirk and I are from southern California, and it had been years since we had eaten at In and Out Burger. Kirk had been craving a good burger since we had arrived in Texas, and I figured that twenty-seven days was a long enough wait. We stopped and savored our meal in Dallas before continuing the trek home. The journey was a bit uncomfortable for Kirk, but overall it went very well.

It was near midnight when we arrived at my parents' house. We would temporarily be living with them while Kirk recovered. I was on the verge of tears when we pulled into their driveway. It had been far too long since I had been able to hug my mom and dad. I got out of the car and we hugged and cried, but only for a minute. I needed to help Kirk out of the car. With someone on each side of him, Kirk stood, with his arms around their shoulders, and walked about twenty steps into the house and to a recliner. These were the first real steps he had taken in almost a month. His first steps were to enter the house we would be calling home.

He had to take another twenty or more steps to get into the bedroom. This was done in the same fashion as before, with someone on either side of him, using them to support his weight and keep him from falling. It was almost a carry both times, but it was such a relief to be home and in a bedroom where there were no nurses or machines in sight. I said goodbye to our son so he could go home and get some sleep before working the next morning, then told my parents goodnight with one last set of hugs. Kirk and I got ready for bed. I was so thankful to finally climb in bed and sleep curled up next to the man I love. I realized at that moment what a tremendous gift that this one simple act was. How many nights had I taken that and him for granted?

We slept like babies that night. I can't remember ever feeling more rested in my life after those nine glorious hours. It felt like waking up on Christmas. I was going to get dressed and go out and my parents would be there; I knew that, within a matter of hours, two of our daughters and our granddaughters would be visiting too. I got up quietly and dressed, but decided to let Kirk sleep. My mom and I went to a friend's house and picked up a wheelchair for Kirk to borrow, along with a walker. My mother had already set up the bathroom with a safety toilet seat and shower chair. We did our best to prepare for the new normal.

We spent the next few days being loved on by our family. We rested a lot, ate good food, and spent hours talking. After just eight days, I noticed that Kirk's wounds were starting to look infected. The incision sites for the ECMO and Impella were right in the fold of the leg, where the thigh meets the pelvic area. When Kirk lay flat, air got to them and it was easy to keep them clean. Since being home, he had been sitting a lot and there was little air flow, so germs began to breed.

I took him to the VA clinic, where we were told he would need to be transferred to a hospital to have a wound debridement. He was admitted into a Tulsa hospital. They were able to surgically clean the Impella site, but the ECMO site was badly infected. When he came out of surgery, it looked like they had taken an ice cream scoop and removed one full scoop of flesh from the top of his thigh. Our new adventure would require a wound vac. This meant packing his open wound with a black medical sponge that encouraged cell growth. Then, it was covered in a giant clear bandage that connected to a small portable vacuum to keep constant suction. This aided in the healing process. We were told that the wound vac would be a part of our lives for three to four months.

After six days in the hospital, Kirk was discharged...again. This time we left with the life vest, the portable wound vac, and a two week supply of IV antibiotics. I had to be taught how to administer medication through a pick line in Kirk's arm. A home health nurse would be coming three times a week to change the dressings on the wound vac. It seemed like things were just not going to get any easier.

We powered through the next two weeks, and finally I administered the final dose of antibiotics to Kirk. The home health nurse would be coming to remove the pick line and we were watching television in the living room. I got up to get a drink when Kirk called my name. He had his first ever nosebleed. Oh the joys of blood thinners! At least we knew they were doing their job. The problem was his nose would not stop bleeding. We tried all of the tips the nurse had suggested. After filling up the trash can with bloody tissue, and making another call to the home health nurse, we headed to the ER.

They shoved something called a rhino rocket up into Kirk's nose. It looked long enough to reach his brain. They left it there for an hour, and his nose still did not stop bleeding. The doctor had to use another style that would require him being admitted to the hospital…again. Three days and two rhino rockets later, we left the hospital for the third time. We wondered if these trips would ever end.

Three weeks were also all it took for his wound to close. We were told three months, and God stepped in and proved once again that His ways are not our ways. The running theme or lesson in every step has been to "watch what God does." I still remember the day that the final dressing came off. The home health nurse told Kirk that he could take a shower. The smile that lit up his face was pure joy. Sponge baths are okay, but absolutely nothing beats a long hot shower. It had been nearly two months since Kirk had been able to take a shower. This was a huge gift.

Without the life vest and wound vac, Kirk was finally able to move around more freely, and we were able to do something we had been really looking forward to. We woke up the following Sunday morning excited for the day. My parents had already left for church. Kirk and I had already decided to get ready and go, but had told nobody. He was still using a wheelchair for distances more than ten to fifteen feet. He chose to walk into the church building that morning. I believe it was close to thirty feet. He walked with his hand on my shoulder for support. He was completely out of breath, but he did it. We were welcomed with smiling faces, and surrounded by friends and family, who had held us both up in prayer for the past months. What an amazing testimony it was for Kirk to walk in that door. Testimonies are such a powerful tool in the hands of believers. They draw people to Christ and strengthen the faith of those who already believe.

Chapter 9

It has been over two years since our lives were so drastically altered. Kirk and I continue to learn and grow daily. God has taught us so many lessons through these trials. He has overwhelmed us with His love and wisdom through it all. We believe that the things He does are meant to be shared with others.

I have learned that God knows what we need before we can even utter the words. In Matthew 6, Jesus tells us that even the birds do not worry about what they will eat or drink. God takes care of each and every need that we have.

When we were in the hospital and I was too heartbroken to even know what to pray, God had already lined up all that I would need. He ministered to me, lifted me, and loved me through it all. Psalms 27:8 (CSV) says, "My heart has heard you say, 'come and talk with me,' And my heart replies 'Lord I am coming.'" We don't even have to utter any words; God hears our hearts. When I didn't know how to pray for my husband and all I could do was place my hands on his chest and cry, my spirit was crying out to save him, and God heard my cries. His love overwhelmed me and it continues to do so.

The second thing that I have learned, and continue to learn daily, is how very much I can trust Him. Psalm 27:1 (CSV) says, "The Lord is my light and my salvation, so why should I be afraid?" I have always said the words, "I trust God," and I always meant them. I really thought that I meant them with all of my heart. You see, it's easy to trust God when your world is unshaken. You do normal things: go to work, make dinner, do laundry, and trust God. Isn't that how most of us approach trust?

We lived in Oklahoma for part of my early years, and living there meant experiencing an occasional tornado. Tornado watches and warnings in the springtime are part of the norm. We would always keep our eye on the weather reports and trust God to protect us. In 1984, when I was thirteen years old, an F5 tornado touched down one Sunday morning in our small town while we were in church. The sirens went off and, when we heard them, the church members jumped into action. Some of them walked around and prayed. One lady got under the grand piano. My dad got our family of four together and prayed for God's protection. I watched, entranced at the scene through the glass doors of our church building. The cars in the parking lot bounced from the force of the winds. Then I heard a sound like a freight train as the tornado, which was half a mile wide, tore through our town. Then there was silence. We trusted God to protect us. Our entire church was protected from the storm's impact, as were our cars. I saw for myself that I could trust God, and He had proven Himself to us in a big way. We drove down the hill from church and saw total devastation. Our town had taken a terrible hit. The National Guard were called in, and Mannford, Oklahoma was declared a disaster area.

I learned that day that I could trust God to protect us, but the level of trust that I gained by watching God bring my husband back to life cannot be learned by going to a Bible study, or even experiencing a tornado. I literally watched with my own eyes the almighty God breathe life back into the man I love. That kind of trust can only be learned by walking through it. You have to keep this in mind as you go through trials and tribulations. God has allowed it for a purpose, and for your good. Most importantly, it is all for His glory. If you look at the situation and get angry or depressed or fail to ask God what His purpose for you is in it, you miss out on the wonderful gifts that He has in store. Yes, it is a gift, because God uses it to teach us to trust him in a way that we won't learn without going through it.

It is a choice to see it. Those ladies in the elevator told me to watch what God does! God wanted me to see Kirk healed. More importantly, He wanted me to see—really see—that He was in complete control and that His plan was to do exceedingly abundantly above all that I could ask or think.

The final lesson that I learned and am still learning and that I would like to share with you is that God has a plan. He had a plan for Kirk and me and it works beautifully. Musically speaking, God puts together the most incredible orchestras. I am currently watching the first snowfall of the winter season. There isn't much snow in Oklahoma. As I watch it fall and begin to cover the ground, this thought came to me. Just like a single snowflake, we are each unique, and have a special purpose. We are each beautiful on our own. When you put us all together, it makes an even more beautiful picture. This is how, as a body of believers, we are supposed to be. We each do our part that God calls us to do, and together we are part of His incredible story.

God has a special plan for Kirk and me, a burning desire that was not present before. This desire is for outreach. We want to reach out to others in whatever way God chooses to lead us. He has begun to open opportunities to us and we know that it is only the beginning. He will lead toward His big plan for us. We started a ministry called Sunset Sunrise Ministries, and yes, there is a Facebook page to go with it. We simply share with others what God teaches us. When God opens doors to share our testimony with others, we always do so willingly. It is simple. We just follow His lead.

We are all created to be a part of God's big plan. Just like an orchestra, if we all participate in the part that God custom made us for, then the outcome is a beautiful symphony that without a doubt gets a standing ovation by God. When you stand and look at it, it is the most breathtaking picture that you can possibly describe. Just like the snow reflects the sunlight, we reflect God's light to the world. When we follow His lead, all of heaven rejoices over us.

The lessons God is teaching require me to see things through different eyes. I can look back now and see that God's hand was in every single thing that took place, down to the smallest details. We need to look at everything in and around us with our spiritual eyes and walk by faith and not by sight. We need to understand that He works everything for good, for those who trust Him. His plans are for our good and not for harm. He is in complete control. He loves us and nothing will ever stop that love.

When Kirk woke up that day in the hospital, he had very little memory of the events that took place. The beginning of the book starts with his words. It is his description of the few bits and pieces of memories he now has of July 23. He does not remember leaving Belize. He doesn't remember being on the airplane. His bits of memories start in Houston Hobby Airport and then pick back up ten days later when he first came off the ventilator.

Since then, he has shared a lot with me. The first thing he told me was that when he cried those nights in the hospital, it was because he didn't understand why he wasn't in heaven. Every part of his being desired to be with the Lord, to be home. He was, and is, so ready whenever it is his time. That stunned me. I didn't feel that same longing. Sure I want to go to heaven when I die, but I had never been in tears over the thought of not being there.

God used Kirk to help that change in me. I started to read all about heaven. In my searching, I gained a much clearer understanding of what it will truly be like. I now look forward with eager expectation to go home whenever God calls me. Kirk's experience is unique. Others have gone through similar experiences, but no two stories are alike. I look at my husband now and see that he is not the same man who got on the airplane to come home with me. God has radically changed him through this. It took him a while to talk about what he experienced when he died. But when he did I was blown away.

He woke up with a tangible experience of heaven. Even though much of his memory is gone from that time, he has clearly has been in the presence of Jesus. He smiles all of the time, and there is a lightness that wasn't there before. He has a tremendous desire to learn as much as God will teach him daily. He always had faith in God, always believed. Now there are countless, noticeable changes to all of us who know him well. He is a man who experienced God in a very real and personal way. Do I believe he was in heaven when he died? Yes, absolutely I do.

Chapter

Kirk and I have had many deep conversations since coming home to Oklahoma. It is best to have him share in his own words what God has laid on his heart as well as what God allowed him to experience.

-Kirk-

One of the biggest questions I have is why do so many Christians cling so tightly to this world? Why do we work so hard for things that do not really matter? For non-Christians, it makes sense to work hard for things, because they have no hope for something more. As Christians, we have the God-given fact of eternity with Him. Ambition is a great thing if you are ambitious for the things God puts in front of you. I see so many Christians with ambition for a big house, or to make a certain amount of money, and they place God in the back seat. Some look for fame, or position in their jobs, or they want recognition without keeping God as the primary focus. That is not how Jesus taught us to live.

He told us to forsake all of that stuff and follow him. That does not mean that we should give up our jobs or houses. It does mean that we should be asking these questions: What does He want me doing? Where does He want me working? We spend so much of our time doing all kinds of things that do not matter in the grand plans that God has for us. Matthew 6:19 (CSV) says, "Don't store up for yourselves treasures on earth, where moth and rust destroy and where thieves break in and steal."

We also fall for the lies that we can do something tomorrow. Well guess what: I have learned in a real way that tomorrow is not a promise. People die young every day; even kids die. God does not promise us tomorrow, but He does promise us eternal life with Him. Where are we building our treasures? As a Christian, who do you really serve?

Why do Christians let greed control them? Sometimes we can be greedy for money, but what about being greedy with our loved ones. We want to keep them here, but God chooses the time for them to go home. Sometimes people resent God or get angry because they lose someone they love, when the reality is, if they know Christ, they should be rejoicing not resenting. They have gone to the most amazing destination, remain in the presence of the Savior, will be there for eternity, and someday you will get to join them. Why would you not want that for them? We should want this for everyone we love. "The one that loves a father or mother more than me is not worthy of me. The one who loves a son or daughter more than me is not worthy of me" (Matthew 10:37 CSV).

Is there really anything in the world that should be more important to us than God? We focus more on whether or not certain people like us, than if God is pleased with us. We will spend every last bit of time we have working overtime in a job we hate just to have extra money for a vacation that is months away. Instead, we should be spending time with those we love most, making sure that we are examples of God to them and telling them about what the Lord has done in our lives. We need to be sure they see Christ in us, are drawn to Him, and know Him and believe.

My way of being an example is to tell others what God did. It is not easy to speak about this and stay true to what I experienced. I don't want to exaggerate anything or embellish it in any way. I want to be as honest as possible. So here goes.

One minute, I was in the dark and the next minute, I was standing on a balcony staring at the water. My hands were resting on the railing and I could feel the wind blowing. At first, it felt like I was back in Belize, but the sun was in the wrong location. The water was so spectacular, so much more beautiful than the water in Belize. I had never seen water with so many colors. The sand was bright and clean and appeared like tiny pearls. Standing there looking at the shoreline, I saw a family walking by. They were having a wonderful time. We looked at each other and there was a connection. When we saw each other, there was a sense of knowing each other, like their names were on the tip of my tongue. I wondered how I knew them, but they were familiar to me. I know they were family, but I am not sure exactly who they were.

At some point after seeing them, I noticed all of the differences about where I was and then I was sure. I was not in Belize. There was this feeling that suddenly took over my attention. The feeling radiated from the sun and caused me to take a knee. With my forearms resting on the railing, I rested my head on my arms like I was praying. I looked at my arms and they were tan and strong. Something was so different. It didn't hurt to kneel; I felt like I was in my twenties again. In fact, nothing hurt at all and I was able to stand back up with no effort. The overwhelming feeling was pure love and it was coming from the sun—or rather the *Son*! I just stood there in awe and I didn't want to leave. I didn't even want to move. I wanted to soak in that feeling and that was all I wanted. Someone started calling my name. I tried to ignore it, but the person continued, and I was suddenly ripped away. The next thing I remember was waking up in the hospital and not knowing how I got there. I had so many questions about where I was and why I was there.

I want to be perfectly honest and clear about this. I am not trying to hurt anybody's feelings, and I understand how what I have to say might, but people are very selfish. My wife had an army of people praying for me to come back and get well. Because of that, I was ripped away from the *best place ever*! I know it was done out of love, but I was taken from the best place ever and I have to share that with you.

Now that I have that out of my system, I woke up mad, angry, and hurt. I was also sad and depressed, and felt total loss. I didn't know how to process why I was blessed by such a small glimpse of paradise and then had to come back here. There are times when I feel that it would have been better if God had sent me to hell, rather than heaven for that short visit. The reason I say that is because coming back here from hell would have been a relief. I would have been thankful to come back. Coming back here after being in heaven is extremely painful. There is absolutely nothing here that compares to it.

It is not that I don't love my family. I love them with all of my heart, but there is no comparison to being there. Now getting back to those first feelings of anger and sadness, I began going over and over things in my head. I asked God, "Do you not love me? Am I not good enough? (The truth is no, I am not.) Did I mess up? What is the purpose of all of this?" Then little by little, He started to show my why I am here...again. Some Christians are better or more responsible at getting their jobs done and doing the Lord's work. They don't procrastinate. The hear Him and they do what He asks. When they finished the job, they are rewarded and get to go home. As for me, I procrastinated and hesitated and I just didn't live my life to the full potential for the Lord. Instead, I lived life striving to meet society's standards. I put the needs and wants of my family above everything else, even God.

Now that my eyes are open, I live my life with the Lord as priority number one, and everything else in my life naturally falls into the proper order.

I am in a place that I never expected to be. I guess you can say that I am at rock bottom, by society's standards. No longer do I have the ability to hold the job I had before. I now have physical limitations that keep me from that. No longer do I have money to do with as I please; God has removed my ability to do it on my own. No longer do I have a home of my own. Human wisdom says that I am down and out. But God has given me a gift. By His standards, I am right where He wants me to be. I am not failing with my faith in God. I am not rock bottom, but standing on the rock that is Jesus and His promises for me. I am more joyful, content, at peace, and thankful than I have ever been in my life. I look forward to what God has planned because He is my source. He provides what I need, and I lack nothing. I now am more fearful or cautious in that I never want to be so successful that I take my eyes off Jesus. I trust Him to lead me where I am to go.

We have our focus all wrong. We need to focus on the eternal not the temporary. We need to focus on pleasing God, not on pleasing humans. We need to focus on being more like Jesus, rather than following the popular trends. And we should be speaking boldly about God and sharing our testimonies, rather than being cowards and afraid to step on people's toes or offend them. Jesus was no coward. He offended people daily by speaking truth to them out of His love for them. We are called to be like Jesus. Don't fear what may happen by choosing to live boldly. As a Marine, I would gladly fight for my brother, or lay down my life to defend this country if called upon.

"I say to you my friends, don't fear those who kill the body, and after that can do nothing more. But I will show you the one to fear: fear him who has the authority to throw people into hell after death. Yes I say to you, this is the one to fear." (Luke 12:4–5 CSV)

We should have the desire to defend and guard our faith in that same way. Bc bold for God—you are not here to live life in fear. 2 Timothy 1:7 (CSV) states, "God has not given us a spirit of fear, but of power, love, and of a sound mind." God is literally telling us not to fear, but to be bold in love and with his wisdom and direction.

Our main goal in this world should be going home to be with our savior, and having Him tell us we did good and remained faithful. If that is really our focus, and our hearts truly desire it, it will be only natural to share that with all of those who we love. We will also want to tell people who God brings across our path about that desire and point them to the one who loves them enough to die in their place. It is all about Jesus. Every test, every trial, every change of plans, all that we are given and all that is taken away, is all for His glory.

The question is this: will we let God show His glory through us? Will we really watch what God does? His divine fingerprints are on it all. He will use us, in each and every situation, as a vessel to show His glory. We just need to be willing to let Him. Don't get angry in troubling situations—look for God in them. When you pray in a situation, have faith like that centurion did for his servant. God will have the victory. If someone we love dies, remember this: that person just got on the express lane to go home. The rest of us are waiting in that long line for our turn. Be glad for the person.

We want to see miracles. Too often we are robbed of seeing God work because we let too many things get in the way of our relationship with Him. We can read his word and pray, and go through all of the right motions, but there is no real desire or hunger for more. Take time to be alone with God and just listen. Ask Him to speak to you and He will. You have to be quiet long enough to hear Him. You have to make that quiet time a priority and just listen. He will speak to you in many ways.

I have learned these past few months to lie in bed before I get up and just listen, and also to talk to God, my spirit talking to His. I do the same at night, before I go to bed. At times, thoughts just rush in and sometimes it's like having a conversation with a person. It is something I look forward to each morning and evening. I also sleep at night with ear buds in. I listen to the Bible on an Audible app. I have asked God to give me knowledge of His Word and from him directly. This is the best way for me to get the Word in there. Through his Word and also His words, He is delivering that wisdom to me.

I have struggled with nightmares for years. Different life experiences have woken me up in a panic. God has used His Word to stop them. Now my dreams are just dreams. God gives me adventures in my sleep and I enjoy them. God is renewing my mind. I am not a talker but a listener. Talking is just not in my character. I am more of an observer of people. I can be in a room full of people talking and have no desire to say a word. I can be in a quiet room and have no need to fill the quiet with my words. However, when God gives you words to share, you must obey. I have never had a desire to preach. I am in no way a speaker. But, I must share this.

Open your eyes. Life here is short, but life with God is forever. My friend Bob told me when I had my first heart issues in Belize that it was not my time. Soon, it will be my time. Do not be fooled into thinking you have a lot of it.

Are you ready? Are you ready to die, to go to heaven? Because ready or not, you will die; it will happen. You can't outrun it. If you are a Christian, do not be afraid of death. It doesn't hurt. Coming back hurts. Being here, we experience pain, but Jesus took the sting out of death. We will all face that moment of judgment. Now is the time to make that choice. Now is that day of reckoning for you. This means that today you can choose to face what you have been avoiding up until this moment. What will you decide?

I think back to those morning bike rides in Belize. God has taught me this.

We all have a sunrise.
We will all have a sunset.
Nobody knows when sunset will be.
I can only imagine
How beautiful my sunset will be.
I look forward to my final sunset
Beyond that I look forward to my greatest sunrise!